THE PRACTICAL STRATEGIES SERIES
IN AUTISM EDUCATION

series editors
FRANCES A. KARNES & KRISTEN R. STEPHENS

Diagnosis and Treatment of Children With Autism Spectrum Disorders

Sarah E. O'Kelley, Ph.D.
Elizabeth McMahon Griffith, Ph.D.
Laura Grofer Klinger, Ph.D.
Sarah Ann McCurry

Routledge
Taylor & Francis Group

NEW YORK AND LONDON

First published 2009 by Prufrock Press Inc.

Published 2021 by Routledge
605 Third Avenue, New York, NY 10017
2 Park Square, Milton Park, Abingdon, Oxon OX14 4RN

Routledge is an imprint of the Taylor & Francis Group, an informa business

ISBN 13: 978-1-59363-372-1 (pbk)

Contents

Series Preface

The Practical Strategies Series in Autism offers teachers, counselors, administrators, parents, and other interested parties up-to-date information on a variety of issues pertaining to the characteristics, diagnosis, treatment, and education of students with autism spectrum disorders. Each guide addresses a focused topic and is written by an individual with authority on the issue. Several guides have been published. Among the titles are:

- *An Introduction to Children With Autism*
- *Diagnosis and Treatment of Children With Autism Spectrum Disorders*
- *Educational Strategies for Children With Autism Spectrum Disorders*

For a current listing of available guides within the series, please contact Prufrock Press at 800-998-2208 or visit http://www.prufrock.com.

Acknowledgements

Support for the literature review contained in this volume was provided by the Alabama Council for Developmental Disabilities through the activities of the Alabama Autism Collaborative Group (AACG) and statewide needs assessment team, of which each author was a member. The authors sincerely acknowledge the AACG members for their comments and input on an earlier version of this document. Special thanks and acknowledgement is offered to Karen Bowen Dahle, Ed.D., for her comments and contributions regarding the integration and understanding of educational law and procedures in framing this review. Additional appreciation is extended to Beverly Mulvihill, Ph.D., for her leadership and coordination of the AACG efforts and for her contributions to the literature review. Finally, we thank Angie Barber, Ph.D., for her comments and contributions regarding the early screening and diagnosis of autism.

Pervasive Developmental Disorders (PDD) are a category of neurodevelopmental disorders that includes diagnoses of autism, Asperger's syndrome, and Pervasive Developmental Disorder Not Otherwise Specified (PDD-NOS), which involve impairments in verbal and nonverbal communication, impaired social skills, and a restricted range of activities and interests (American Psychiatric Association [APA], 2000). The term *autism spectrum disorders* (ASD) is a relatively new term meant to convey the heterogeneity of symptom presentation and functional impairment in individuals with PDD (Schopler, 2001). The term ASD also implies that these disorders occur along a continuum or "spectrum." The level of skills and impairments varies across diagnosis and across individuals, as does the response to intervention. For example, recent estimates suggest that approximately 40–60% of individuals with ASD also have mental retardation (see Fombonne, 2005, for a review; Centers for Disease Control and Prevention, 2007) while the other 40–60% have average or above-average intelligence. Currently, the cause of ASD is known to be genetic with likely gene-environment interactions due to early environmental insult (e.g., hypotheses include an infection in utero or maternal exposure to a toxin). Although the genetic cause of autism in some individuals is known (e.g., related to genetic disorders including Fragile X or Tuberous Sclerosis), the exact genetic cause is unknown in the majority of individuals with autism (see O'Roak & State, 2008, for a review). Autism spectrum disorders occur in all racial and ethnic groups and in persons from all economic backgrounds. The gender ratio is approximately 3–4 males for every 1 female with ASD. Prevalence estimates are rising dramatically, with current rates estimated to be 1 in 150 (Centers for Disease Control and Prevention, 2007). Thus, this group of disorders represents the fastest growing neurodevelopmental disorder of childhood, and the Centers for Disease Control and Prevention considers ASD to be an "urgent public health concern."

This publication examines the current available research regarding screening, diagnosis, and treatment of children with a known or suspected ASD. One of the challenges of this review is to summarize the large number of academic publications related to these topics in an easily accessible format; thus, this volume should be considered solely a summary of these topics. In addition, it is of note that although this series and volume focus on children with ASD, as does much of the current research literature, ASD is a *lifelong* disorder that impacts multiple domains of functioning for the individual and his or her family, and the effects of the diagnosis vary across the lifespan.

Screening and Diagnosis for Autism Spectrum Disorders in Children With Suspected Developmental Delays

Factors Impacting Early and Accurate Recognition and Diagnosis

There often is a significant delay between initial parent concerns and an autism diagnosis. In a nationwide Centers for Disease Control and Prevention (2007) study in the United States, parents in most states reported that they were concerned about their child's development before his or her second birthday. Studies tracking the early development of ASD symptoms indicate that social communication deficits (Osterling, Dawson, & Munson, 2002; Wetherby, Brosnan-Maddox, Peace, & Newton, 2008) and repetitive behaviors (Baranek, 1999; Ozonoff et al., 2008) are present by 12 months of age. Parents usually bring their initial concerns to medical providers such as pediatricians. Unfortunately, caregivers report that pediatricians often lack the training necessary to offer additional education about the autism diagnosis or to offer evidence-based treatment recommendations (Myers, Johnson, & the Council on Children With Disabilities, 2007). Due to a lack of pediatrician training and the limited availability of autism resources in most locations, the average age of diagnosis in the United States and the United Kingdom is 3 to

4 years (Chakrabarti & Fombonne, 2005; Filipek et al., 1999). The average age of diagnosis varies from state to state, and greater delays in early screening and diagnosis exist for minority children and children living in poverty or rural environments. Children in these groups often are evaluated at a later age and are more likely to receive an incorrect diagnosis (Mandell, Ittenback, Levy, & Pinto-Martin, 2007; Mandell, Novak, & Zubritsky, 2005).

The age of first diagnosis also is related to the ASD subtype and level of developmental delays that the child displays. Children who have average or better intelligence or fewer observable symptoms of ASD tend to be diagnosed later than children with more severe symptoms and developmental delays. For example, in a statewide survey conducted in Pennsylvania, children with classic autism, which presumably involves a greater quantity of observable behavioral characteristics, received a diagnosis at an average age of 3.1 years. However, in children whose diagnoses indicate that there were fewer observable symptoms, such as children with PDD-NOS or Asperger's syndrome, diagnoses were obtained at an average age of 3.9 years and 7.2 years, respectively (Mandell et al., 2005).

This delay between parents' first concerns and an accurate diagnosis of ASD is cause for concern, as researchers have suggested that early intervention leads to better long-term outcomes. For example, children with ASD who participated in intensive early intervention services before 3 ½ years of age were reported to have significantly better outcomes than children with ASD who did not receive services until 5 years of age (Fenske, Zalenski, Krantz, & McClannahan, 1985; Harris & Handleman, 2000). Furthermore, given the strong genetic components, early detection and diagnosis of ASD in a child provides an opportunity to educate the family about the increased likelihood of this diagnosis among siblings and other family members (Johnson, Myers, & the Council on Children With Disabilities, 2007). Identification of ASD ideally would prompt additional evaluation to determine whether there is an identifiable cause (e.g., genetic syndrome) and to monitor comorbid disorders or symptoms (e.g., intellectual disability or seizure disorders).

Professional Guidelines for Screening and Diagnosis

In response to the known delays between first concerns and formal diagnosis, practice parameters for the screening and diagnosis of ASD have been published by a number of professional organizations, including the American Academy of Neurology (Filipek et al., 1999, 2000), the American Academy of Child and Adolescent Psychiatry (Volkmar, Cook, Pomeroy, Realmuto, & Tanguay, 1999), and the American Academy of Pediatrics (Johnson et al., 2007). Across these published guidelines and recommendations, a consistent set of suggestions emerges:

- education for healthcare providers (e.g., pediatricians, physician assistants, nurses) and early childhood education professionals (e.g., daycare providers) regarding normative developmental milestones and early "red flags" for ASD;
- routine early screening for developmental delays at well-child healthcare visits, including symptoms of ASD or delays in communication and social skills;
- interdisciplinary diagnostic evaluations for children whose early screening suggests possible developmental delays; and
- evaluations for ASD conducted by professionals with specific expertise in ASD that include psychological, speech/language, and medical evaluations.

The American Academy of Neurology (Filipek et al., 1999, 2000) provided a sensible three-step process that progresses from routine screening of all young children to obtaining information about warning signs specific to ASD that indicate a need for further evaluation and diagnosis. These guidelines can be practically incorporated into existing models of pediatric care. The guidelines suggest the following:

Step 1: Routine Developmental Surveillance. Providers are encouraged to suggest immediate further developmental evaluation, including ASD screening, if any of the following concerns are noted:
- no babbling, pointing, or gestures at 12 months;
- no single words at 16 months;
- no spontaneous, nonechoed two-word phrases by 24 months; or
- any loss of language or social skills at any age.

Step 2: Screening Specifically for ASD. If concerns arise during the routine developmental screening, the following recommendations are made for screening specifically for ASD:
- completion of an ASD-specific screening measure; and
- medical evaluation to rule out hearing loss, visual impairment, and/or other physiological anomalies.

Step 3: Diagnostic Evaluation. If concerns arise during the screening for ASD symptoms (i.e., significant items are endorsed that suggest a possibility of ASD), a referral for a comprehensive ASD diagnostic evaluation is recommended.

Early Screening: Primary Care and General Population Screening

Studies regarding early screening have found this strategy to decrease the lag in time between parental concerns and early intervention services. For example, Hix-Small, Marks, Squires, and Nickel (2007) used the Ages and Stages Questionnaire (ASQ; Bricker, Squires, & Mounts, 1995; Squires, Bricker, & Twombly, 2002) to screen for ASD at 12- and 24-month well-child visits. They reported that 67% of children identified with delays on the ASQ were not identified by their pediatricians. These findings highlight the impact early screening could have on children receiving the early intervention services they need. In addition to regular developmental screening, the American Academy of Pediatrics (Johnson et al., 2007) recommended that all children receive ASD-specific screening during routine well-child pediatrician visits at 18 and 24 months.

Although there is a growing consensus about the need for developmental and ASD-specific screening within the primary care office, there is a lack of consensus regarding the most appropriate screening instrument, particularly whether screening should (a) occur at a more general developmental level, (b) be specific for an ASD, or (c) assess for both ASD and other related communication delays. Instruments are available for each of these purposes. A selection of the most popular screening instruments is described below. This is not a comprehensive list, but it does provide a guide to the types of instruments that currently are available. For a more comprehensive discussion of screening instruments, see a review by Johnson and colleagues (2007), a recent special issue of the journal *Autism* (September 2008) that reviewed ASD screening instruments, and Zwaigenbaum and colleagues (2009).

Ages and Stages Questionnaire (ASQ)

The ASQ (Bricker et al., 1995; Squires et al., 2002) is a broad-based measure of developmental milestones in infants and young children from 4 to 48 months of age. It is a 30-item primary caregiver questionnaire that takes approximately 10 to 15 minutes to complete and screens for communication, gross motor, fine motor, problem-solving, and personal-social skills. It is a fast, reliable method of screening for a wide variety of developmental disorders. The ASQ is available for purchase from the publisher.

Communication and Symbolic Behavior Scales Developmental Profile Infant-Toddler Checklist (CSBS DP ITC)

The CSBS DP ITC (Wetherby & Prizant, 2002) is a 24-item caregiver questionnaire designed for use in a primary care setting as a screener for autism and related communication delays. Standard scores are available for 6- to 24-month-old infants and toddlers and it takes 5 to 10 minutes to complete. The ITC measures seven language predictors: emotion and use of eye gaze, use of communication, use of gestures, use of sounds, use of words, understanding of words, and use of objects. Although it is designed to screen for a number of communication disorders, it is successful at detecting ASD. In a sample of 5,000 children, the CSBS ITC successfully identified children later diagnosed with ASD at high rates during the 15- to 24-month age intervals (Wetherby et al., 2008). Specifically, the success of accurately identifying children with autism without incorrectly identifying children who did not have autism was approximately 76% (i.e., positive predictive value). The CSBS ITC is available free to providers at http://firstwords.fsu.edu/toddlerChecklist.html.

Modified Checklist for Autism in Toddlers (M-CHAT)

The M-CHAT (Dumont-Mathieu & Fein, 2005; Robins, Fein, Barton, & Green, 2001) is a 23-item caregiver questionnaire designed for use in a primary care setting as a screener for autism-specific symptoms. It is appropriate for children between 16 and 48 months of age and takes approximately 10 minutes to complete. The follow-up caregiver phone interview takes approximately 15 minutes to administer. The M-CHAT specifically assesses symptoms associated with early signs of autism, including a failure to respond to name, poor eye contact, and failure to follow another person's nonverbal cues. In a recent study of approximately 3,800 16- to 30-month-old children, the M-CHAT was most successful at screening for autism during a well-child visit if it was combined with a follow-up caregiver phone interview (Kleinman et al., 2008). Specifically, the success of accurately identifying children with autism without incorrectly identifying children who did not have autism was approximately 11% (positive predictive value). When a brief follow-up phone interview was conducted, the rate increased to 65%. The M-CHAT is available free to providers at http://www.firstsigns.org/downloads/m-chat.PDF.

Additional Measures

There are additional measures available for the purpose of screening that have been discussed in recent reviews that are not reviewed here, such as the Pervasive Developmental Disorders Screening Test-II (PDDST-II; Siegel, 2004). However, to date, the PDDST-II has not been studied in a primary care setting sample, which limits comparison with measures such as the CSBS ITC and the M-CHAT.

Early Screening: At-Risk Early Service Provider Settings

After a child has been identified as being at-risk for ASD based on a primary care screener (i.e., a Level 1 screener), early interventionists should incorporate an autism-specific screener (i.e., a Level 2 screener) that allows measurement of features such as social interaction, nonverbal communication, and repetitive behaviors. Level 2 screening instruments are specifically designed to follow a negative outcome from an initial Level 1 screening instrument but are not widely available for practical use.

Level 2 screening instruments for ASD include the Screening Tool for Autism in Two-Year-Olds (STAT; Stone, Coonrod, & Ousley, 2000; Stone, Coonrod, Turner, & Pozdol, 2004; Stone, McMahon, & Henderson, 2008) and the Systematic Observation of Red Flags for Autism Spectrum Disorders in Young Children (SORF; Wetherby et al., 2004). These Level 2 screeners typically involve the administration of specific probes to evaluate the presences of autism-specific symptoms. For example, the examiner may point to an object to see if the child can follow the point. These instruments typically require training in administration and scoring. The STAT, in particular, is appropriate for administration within an early intervention setting to detect autism-specific symptoms. The STAT is a structured play session consisting of 12 items measuring imitation, play, and communication skills. The STAT was developed for assessment of children from 24 to 36 months of age, although a recent exploratory study (Stone et al., 2008) demonstrated its use with children under 24 months. The positive predictive value for correctly identifying children between 12 and 23 months of age was .56, and the negative predictive value (those correctly identified as *not* having ASD) was .97.

When smaller age intervals were examined, the use of the STAT to identify children with ASD over 14 months of age appeared stronger than in younger children.

In addition to the use of Level 2 screeners in an at-risk, early intervention setting, it is important to measure autism-specific behaviors including social skills, nonverbal communication (gestures, eye gaze), and repetitive behaviors to assist in developing appropriate goals and to measure intervention effectiveness. Although many early intervention programs measure success by IQ and language gains, few programs have used these autism-specific symptoms to measure success (Matson, 2007). In addition to the ASD-specific screening tools discussed above (CSBS ITC, M-CHAT, PDDST), the following three tools were identified that evaluate communication, behavior, and play skills that are associated with ASD.

Communication and Symbolic Behavior Scales Developmental Profile (CSBS DP)

The CSBS DP (Wetherby & Prizant, 2002) is a brief play assessment appropriate for 6- to 24-month-old children that measures spontaneous communication, language comprehension, play, and repetitive behavior. Raw scores are converted to Symbolic, Social, and Speech composite standard scores. The CSBS DP also has a companion scale to measure repetitive behaviors demonstrated during the evaluation.

Early Social-Communication Scales (ESCS)

The ESCS (Mundy et al., 2003) is a brief play assessment appropriate for 8- to 30-month-old children that measures joint attention, behavioral requests, and social interaction.

Ages and Stages Questionnaires: Social Emotional (ASQ: SE)

The ASQ: SE (Squires et al., 2002) is a parent questionnaire appropriate for 6- to 60-month-old children that measures self-regulation, compliance, affect, adaptive behaviors, and social interaction.

Autism spectrum disorders are by definition *pervasive* and *developmental*, which implies that many areas of an individual's development are affected, including social development, verbal and nonverbal communication skills, age-appropriate play skills, and cognitive development (APA, 2000). Thus, a thorough and accurate diagnosis of ASD requires an assessment of each of these domains and typically requires an interdisciplinary team approach including at least a psychological evaluation and a speech/language evaluation (Klin, Saulnier, Tsatsanis, & Volkmar, 2005; National Research Council, 2001; Ozonoff, Goodlin-Jones, & Solomon, 2007). Because there is no medical test for ASD, a conclusive diagnosis is based on a detailed history as well as behavioral observations. It is crucial that the interdisciplinary evaluation be conducted by a team of professionals with expertise in ASD and related disorders (National Research Council, 2001). Obtaining detailed information about each domain of functioning by professionals versed in ASD allows for accurate differential diagnosis between ASD and developmental language disorders, global developmental delay, and other similar disorders of childhood. The final diagnosis of an ASD typically is provided by a professional with relevant training in the *Diagnostic and Statistical Manual of Mental Disorders-Text Revision* (*DSM-IV-TR*; APA, 2000) or *International Statistical Classification of Diseases and Related Health Problems, 10th Revision* (*ICD-10*; World Health Organization, 1994).

Guidelines provided by the American Academy of Neurology (Filipek et al., 1999, 2000) and the American Academy of Pediatrics (Johnson et al., 2007) recommend similar essential elements for the comprehensive evaluation of children suspected of having ASD: (a) a detailed clinical interview with a caregiver with an emphasis on symptom areas specific to ASD; (b) behavioral observations structured to assess for ASD-specific symptoms; (c) a psychological evaluation, including measures of developmental/intellectual and adaptive functioning (see Klinger, O'Kelley, & Mussey, 2009, for a review); (d) speech, language, and communication assessment (see Paul & Wilson, 2009, for a review); (e) medical assessment by a developmental pediatrician or neurologist, including medical history and a possible neurological evaluation; and (f) assessment of the caregivers' knowledge of ASD, coping skills, and available resources and supports. Although not considered essential, due to the sensory motor difficulties present in ASD, it often is beneficial to include an occupational and/or physical therapist on the diagnostic team.

ASD-Specific Diagnostic Instruments

Until recently, the diagnosis of ASD has been based on clinician observation and intuition rather than a score on a standardized instrument. However, more objective diagnostic measures are now available. The "gold-standard" diagnostic instruments for research and clinical purposes are the Autism Diagnostic Interview-Revised (ADI-R; Le Couteur, Lord, & Rutter, 2003; Lord, Rutter, & Le Couteur, 1994) and the Autism Diagnostic Observation Schedule (ADOS; Lord et al., 2000; Lord, Rutter, DiLavore, & Risi, 1999). These instruments have significantly increased the ability to diagnose children with ASD with good reliability.

Autism Diagnostic Interview-Revised (ADI-R)

The ADI-R (Le Couteur et al., 2003; Lord et al., 1994) is a semistructured caregiver interview appropriate for individuals between 18 months of age and adulthood. The interview focuses on the individual's social skills, communication skills, and the presence of any restricted and repetitive behaviors. Because diagnostic symptoms change across the lifespan, an ADI-R classification of ASD is based on caregiver report of symptoms during the preschool years when symptoms tend to be the most severe and differentiated from other developmental disorders. However, current behaviors also are assessed to obtain an accurate picture of each individual's current skills. This is a lengthy interview; the short version takes approximately 1½ hours to administer. Because it is so lengthy, many general practitioners find the ADI-R difficult to administer in their daily practice. However, it typically is included in an ASD assessment in clinical settings specializing in ASD.

Autism Diagnostic Observation Schedule-Generic (ADOS)

While the ADI-R provides the "long view" of the individual's development and functioning, the ADOS can be considered a "snapshot" of his or her current behavior and skills. The ADOS (Lord et al., 1999, 2000) is a semistructured play session (or conversation for adults) that creates an environment in which to assess an individual's social skills, communication skills, and the presence of restricted or repetitive behaviors. The ADOS takes approximately 30–45 minutes to administer and is appropriate for individuals from 2 years of age through adulthood; a developmental level of 18 months is necessary for standardized use and interpretation.

There are four different ADOS modules based on the individual's developmental level and current language skills. Module 1 is appropriate for nonverbal individuals, Module 2 is for those using phrase speech, Module 3 is for children and adolescents with fluent language, and Module 4 is designed for adults with fluent language. The materials in the first two modules are more appropriate for young children (e.g., bubbles, balloons, a set of family dolls), the third module has materials of interest for school-aged children and young adolescents (e.g., books, markers, action figures), and the fourth module does not use toys but relies more on conversational activities. Based on behaviors during the session, a series of algorithm items are rated to yield a classification of Autism, Autism Spectrum, or non-spectrum.

The original ADOS scoring algorithm and classifications were based only on social and communication skills because repetitive behaviors and restricted interests were less likely to be observed during a short period of time. During ADOS observation, if repetitive behaviors and restricted interests are observed, the examiner can feel confident that they are present. If behaviors in this symptom area are not observed, a caregiver interview is necessary to assess these behaviors rather than incorrectly assuming these behaviors do not occur, thereby limiting diagnostic accuracy. However, a recent revised scoring algorithm includes scores related to repetitive behaviors and interests (Gotham et al., 2008). This revised algorithm has a greater predictive value (i.e., sensitivity of the measure to yield a classification predictive of eventual diagnosis) than the previous algorithm. Because of the difficulty in assessing repetitive behaviors and interests, a parent interview is an important component of making an accurate diagnosis, and it is not recommended that the ADOS be used in isolation for diagnosing ASD.

ASD-Specific Rating Scales

Both the ADI-R and the ADOS must be administered by a professional who has had extensive training in the administration, scoring, and interpretation of these measures. Further, use of the ADI-R often is precluded by time constraints in clinical settings. There are a variety of less intensive instruments available that may be useful in clinical diagnosis of ASD, mostly in the form of caregiver questionnaires. However, thus far, the ADI-R and ADOS are superior in terms of gathering and summarizing information to guide an accurate diagnosis. Although it is beyond the scope of this review to describe each of the available rating scales, a review of two instruments with good empirical support is provided. Recent reviews by Ozonoff et al. (2007) and Naglieri and Chambers (2009) are good resources for a more comprehensive discussion of caregiver and teacher rating scales.

Social Communication Questionnaire (SCQ)

The SCQ (Rutter, Bailey, & Lord, 2003) is a 40-item caregiver-completed questionnaire developed to screen for communication skills, social functioning, and restrictive and repetitive patterns of behavior that may indicate the presence of ASD. The SCQ is based on *DSM-IV* diagnostic criteria for autism, Asperger's syndrome, and Pervasive Developmental Disorder, Not Otherwise Specified. Respondents circle *yes* or *no* to indicate whether each behavior has been observed in the individual being assessed. There are both lifetime and current versions of this scale. The SCQ is appropriate for children with a mental age of at least 2 years and a chronological age of 4 years and takes approximately 10 minutes to complete. Correlations between the subdomain and total scores on the SCQ and ADI-R range from .31 to .71 (Berument, Rutter, Lord, Pickles, & Bailey, 1999). The SCQ is useful as a screening instrument and as a measure of ASD symptom severity (see Naglieri & Chambers, 2009, for a more comprehensive review).

Social Responsiveness Scale (SRS)

The SRS (Constantino & Gruber, 2005) is a 65-item questionnaire developed to measure social skills, communication, and repetitive or stereotyped behavior. The SRS is appropriate for children between the ages of 4 and 18 years and a preschool version currently is being developed. There are separate caregiver and teacher rating scales that each take approximately 15 minutes to complete. Behaviors are rated on a Likert scale. Cut-off scores are provided for use of the SRS as either a population-based screening measure or for use as a screening and diagnostic tool when children are suspected of having ASD. In addition to a total T score, subscale scores of Social Awareness, Social Cognition, Social Communication, Social Motivation, and Autistic Mannerisms may be calculated. Constantino and colleagues (2003) reported that all children receiving ADI-R scores above the clinical cut-off also had elevated SRS scores. Thus, the SRS is useful as a screening instrument and as a measure of ASD symptom severity (see Naglieri & Chambers, 2009, for a more comprehensive review).

Age and Reliable Diagnosis

Professionals and parents both express concerns about whether an accurate diagnosis can be made at an early age. Although the symptoms of ASD are present by 12 months of age (Baranek, 1999; Osterling et al., 2002; Ozonoff et al., 2008; Wetherby et al., 2008), there are very few diagnostic instruments available for evaluating possible ASD in the second year of life and few studies have examined the accuracy of diagnoses given at this age (Brian et al., 2008). According to the ADOS manual, it may be used with children below the 18-month developmental level but results should be interpreted with caution.

In a study following the development of an at-risk group of infants (e.g., siblings of children with ASD), Brian and colleagues (2008) used the ADOS and the Autism Observation Scale for Infants (AOSI; Bryson, McDermott, Rombough, Brian, & Zwaigenbaum, 2008) to identify behavioral markers at 18 months that were related to a diagnosis at 36 months. They reported that social, behavioral, and temperamental symptoms at 18 months were associated with a diagnosis of ASD at 36 months of age. However, only 56% of children diagnosed with ASD at 36 months were identified accurately at 18 months of age based on the presence of these symptoms. Brian and colleagues concluded that the diagnosis of ASD at 18 months remains a significant challenge for researchers and clinicians.

Studies examining the accuracy of diagnoses at 2 years of age have been much more promising (Stone et al., 2000; Wetherby et al., 2004). Studies using the ADOS (Lord et al., 2006) and the STAT (Turner, Stone, Pozdol, & Coonrod, 2006) have reported that more than 85% of children diagnosed with ASD at 2 years of age retained this diagnosis at 4 years of age. Thus, at present the research suggests that an experienced clinician can make a reliable diagnosis as early as 2 years of age.

Diagnosing ASD Subtypes

There are differences in opinion regarding the capacity of professionals to differentiate reliably among different diagnoses within the autism spectrum. It is likely that the next revision of the *DSM* will not distinguish between or label specific subtypes but will reflect what has been learned about autism as a *spectrum* disorder. Indeed, our gold standard diagnostic instruments do not differentiate between the ASD subtypes. The ADOS diagnosis is either "autism" or "autism spectrum" and the ADI-R diagnosis is "autism." The difficulty of differentiating between ASD subtypes is particularly evident when differentiating between children with high functioning autism and Asperger's syndrome.

According to our current diagnostic system (*DSM-IV-TR*; APA, 2000), Asperger's Disorder is defined by the presence of impaired reciprocal social skills and the presence of restricted behaviors and interests in individuals who have average intelligence and who did not have a history of language delay (i.e., single words by 2 years and phrases by 3 years). Individuals with a history of language delay, regardless of their current level of language skills, cannot be given a diagnosis of Asperger's Disorder. Research comparing the diagnoses of Asperger's Disorder and high functioning autism provides mixed evidence about whether these are indeed separate disorders, as the long-term outcome data are similar for both groups (Ozonoff, South, & Miller, 2000).

Given this debate about how to differentiate between ASD subtypes and whether these subtypes represent different diagnoses, some argue that an emphasis on which diagnosis within the autism spectrum is applicable for a certain child is not imperative. Instead, it may be more important to know about the specific skills, strengths, and weaknesses of the individual.

Cognitive Assessment in Autism Spectrum Disorders

Cognitive testing is a recommended part of an interdisciplinary diagnostic evaluation (Filipek et al., 1999; Johnson et al., 2007). Klin et al. (2005) described developmental testing for infants and preschool-aged children and intellectual assessment for school-aged children as a frame for interpreting the results of diagnostic testing. This "frame" can be used to evaluate whether a child's social and communication delays are greater than expected given the child's developmental level or whether they are equivalent to the child's developmental level. In order to receive a diagnosis of ASD, a child's social and communicative skills must be delayed below a child's developmental level. Cognitive assessment also can play a role in diagnosing Asperger's syndrome, which by definition requires that no clinically significant delays in language, cognitive functioning, and adaptive behavior be present.

The traditional standardized assessment paradigm often is a challenge for children with ASD and for the examiner administering the assessment. Thus, the examiner often needs to structure the session using schedules and rewards to maintain motivation and decrease behavioral difficulties (see Klinger et al., 2009, for ideas on how to structure an intellectual assessment). At a minimum, the examiner should have experience administering intellectual assessments to children and have some knowledge about how the symptoms of ASD may interfere with test administration and performance. Ideally, the examiner will have experience interacting with individuals with ASD, and additional understanding of the symptoms and treatment approaches for ASD will assist the examiner in choosing an appropriate test and structuring the testing session to ensure that the child's performance is representative of his or her true abilities. The choice of an intellectual assessment depends on the child's chronological age, mental age, language abilities, and severity of autism symptoms. It is beyond the scope of this volume to review specific developmental and intellectual assessment instruments; the reader is referred to a recent review of these issues by Klinger et al. (2009).

Supporting Families Following a Diagnosis

The American Academy of Pediatrics (Myers et al., 2007) recommends that after receiving a diagnosis, caregivers should be encouraged to make use of natural supports, such as their spouses, family members, friends, neighbors, or church members. Additionally, the American Academy of Pediatrics recommends that medical or psychological personnel should provide education about formal supports including education and support networks (e.g., Autism Society of America and Autism Speaks) and publicly funded, state-administered programs such as early intervention, special education, vocational and residential/living services, and respite services.

In a recent study of mothers' responses to learning of their child's diagnosis, Wachtel and Carter (2008) reported that mothers who were more emotionally resolved about their child's diagnosis and resisted self-blame were more likely to spend time with their children in activities characterized by greater reciprocity and mutual enjoyment. The authors suggested that prior to involving parents in their child's treatment, it was important for clinicians to focus on issues related to diagnosis and acceptance. Clinicians also should be aware of how multicultural differences impact the diagnosis and understanding of ASD, including how linguistic differences affect how families understand the diagnosis, particularly when their native language does not have a word for autism or the related concepts (Wilder, Dyches, Obiakor, & Algozzine, 2004).

Treatment Approaches for Children
With Autism Spectrum Disorders (ASD)

The Need for ASD-Specific Interventions

Children typically learn by watching and imitating others, and they respond to social praise and attention when learning new skills. However, children with ASD rarely learn by imitating other people (Rogers & Williams, 2006) and they "spend much less time in focused and socially directed activity when in unstructured situations than do other children" (National Research Council, 2001, p. 220). Thus, children with ASD are learning less in the context of their daily lives than their peers with typical development and will therefore require intensive targeted intervention. At the same time, the autism spectrum presents a unique cluster of symptoms and behaviors that are not well addressed by programs implemented to address other developmental disorders. Standard interventions' reliance on social relatedness and typical patterns of motivation, as well as their generally low intensity level (Howlin, 1998), are not well-suited for individuals with ASD. Instead, interventions that are specifically tailored to the unique symptoms of ASD, as well as those that can flexibly address each individual's differences in skills and presentation, will be required. Given the high level of need, it is very important to use treatments that have a solid research foundation so that time and effort spent in training and implementation is not wasted on programs that ultimately do not make a difference for the children and their families.

Cautions on Choosing Interventions

Because the evidence base has been difficult to interpret and this area has not been adequately researched, families and professionals often try therapy approaches that are considered experimental. Green (1996a) and Herbert, Sharp, and Gaudiano (2002) recommended the following guidelines when considering treatment options: Consumers should be wary of treatments involving: (a) grandiose claims (e.g., those stating "miraculous" or "cure"), (b) underlying theories that are not based in generally accepted science, (c) claims to treat multiple unrelated disorders, (d) anecdotes and testimonials rather than good research and real science, (e) promotions primarily via Internet and private publications, and (f) financial gain for promoters.

Pseudoscience, which refers to information that pretends to be scientific, is abundant in the area of ASD (Green, 2001; Herbert & Sharp, 2001). A simple Internet search using terms of "autism" and "treatment" would certainly yield a wide and varied range (at the time of this writing, there were more than 600,000 results) of seemingly effective and promising intervention approaches, but unfortunately many of the results could be considered pseudoscience. The opportunity to take advantage of families of children with ASD is very high, with families typically trying between seven and nine different therapies (Goin-Kochel & Mackintosh, 2007). There also is potential for a large placebo effect among those participating in treatment, especially if the treatment is expensive (Herbert et al., 2002). Specifically, it is possible that when treatment effects are observed or reported, it is not the treatment itself that is driving changes in behavior but rather the fact that a treatment was introduced. In situations where this occurs, it is likely that *any* treatment would have produced the same or similar effects.

When choosing an intervention approach, families and providers are cautioned that it is not the brand name of the program that should be promoted and sought at present, but rather the *core key elements* that have been demonstrated to be effective. Although the evidence base remains somewhat limited, general conclusions about common effective elements across the lifespan are possible. A summary of these conclusions are outlined in the following sections, and examples of interventions are briefly reviewed.

Current Evidence Base

Much of the current literature regarding treatment of any disorder or disability focuses on an effort to establish empirical support to identify evidence-based treatments. Indeed, educational interventions based on this type of rigorous scientific study are mandated by the Individuals With Disabilities Education Improvement Act (IDEA; 2006) and the No Child Left Behind Act (NCLB; 2001). The precise definition of adequate evidence varies slightly between groups of professionals. However, most groups agree that in order to be considered an evidence-based treatment, studies must be published in a peer-reviewed scientific journal using accepted, high-quality research designs, and the intervention must have been studied by multiple researchers and be associated with both statistically significant and clinically significant improvements. The adequate level of methodological rigor and the specific numbers of different studies varies by professional group. The National Autism Center (see Resources section at the end of this volume) definition of evidence-based practice also includes an emphasis on the values of the family and the need for professional judgment and data-based decision making to address the needs of each individual when providing interventions.

Although there is scientific evidence that interventions with individuals with ASD do cause change in symptoms and behavior, more rigorous scientific studies are needed, particularly cross-program comparisons to determine whether one specific program is superior to another (Goldstein, 2002; Lord et al., 2005; McConnell, 2002; Smith et al., 2007). It has proven difficult to obtain a solid evidence base for comprehensive treatment programs or "packages," which generally represent a combination of treatment elements and practices. At present, only Lovaas' comprehensive treatment (Lovaas, 1987; McEachin, Smith, & Lovaas, 1993) meets the most rigorous criteria for being evidence-based, although others are beginning to build more research support (Rogers & Vismara, 2008). Given the difficulty of rigorously examining comprehensive programs and the paucity of research comparing one comprehensive program to another, researchers and clinicians have turned to analyzing the underlying elements or practices that lead to successful intervention.

Common elements or aspects of successful intervention programs were first outlined by professionals, and more recently specific practices or techniques have been identified. The following list outlines the critical elements for intervention during the early years as determined by a number of published reviews (Dawson & Osterling, 1997; Koegel, Koegel, & McNerney, 2001; Myers et al., 2007; National Research Council, 2001; Rogers, 1998, 1999; Schreibman, 2000).

Specific critical elements of intervention include:
- implementation as soon as an ASD diagnosis is seriously considered;
- implementation by highly trained staff who not only have an understanding of the features of ASD but also have training and background in ASD-specific techniques of intervention;
- family involvement and parent education;
- individualized attention (1:1 or very small groups such as 1:3 teacher to student ratio) provided in frequent intervals;
- inclusion with peers with typical development as appropriate in working toward goals;

- a highly structured and supportive environment and routine;
- generalization of skills across environments and working in the natural environment;
- intensive, active engagement in planned programming for more than 25 hours per week, 12 months per year;
- systematic, planned, developmentally appropriate instruction;
- working toward specific individualized goals and objectives;
- ongoing assessment of progress (i.e., at least every 3 months) and adaptation of programming if adequate progress is not being attained; and
- problem behaviors should be addressed in a positive manner and in context, with a focus on developing replacement behaviors.

Skill areas to target in successful intervention curricula include:
- functional, spontaneous communication (verbal, non-verbal, symbolic);
- receptive language;
- social instruction that is appropriate to the child's reference age group;
- imitation;
- play skills, including those involving and requiring peer interaction;
- attention to the environment and response to appropriate motivators;
- cognitive skills taught in context to improve generalization;
- fine and gross motor skills;
- independent organizational skills (e.g., completing tasks, asking for help, following instructions);
- functional academic skills when appropriate; and
- self-help and adaptive skills.

Most recently, the National Professional Development Center (NPDC) on Autism Spectrum Disorders (see Resources section at the end of this volume) and the National Autism Center's National Standards Project began developing full reports reviewing the literature from the past 50 years. Although reports are expected from these groups shortly, updates will continue in the years to come as further progress is made. Reports will include the evidence base for practices that appear to be most effective in intervention with individuals with ASD, as well as indications for their use and specifics on how to implement them to achieve fidelity. In an effort to disseminate information regarding treatment strategies, the NPDC is working with the Ohio Center for Autism and Low Incidence Disorders (OCALI) to develop Web-based modules that will become available to the public (see Resources section at the end of this volume). At present, the NPDC lists the following practices as having an adequate evidence base for use with individuals with ASD (Tuchman-Ginsburg & Shaw, 2008):

- behavioral strategies (prompting, time delay, reinforcement, task analysis, and chaining);
- computer-aided instruction;
- differential reinforcement;
- discrete trial training;
- extinction;
- functional behavior assessment;
- functional communication training;
- naturalistic interventions;
- parent-implemented intervention;
- peer-mediated instruction/intervention;
- Picture Exchange Communication System (PECS);
- pivotal response training;
- response interruption/redirection;
- self-management;
- social narratives;
- social skills training groups;
- stimulus control/environmental modification;

- structured work systems;
- video modeling;
- visual supports; and
- VOCA/SGD (speech generating devices).

In addition to those approaches that were developed specifically for children with ASD, the use of interventions that have evidence-based support in treating other disorders (e.g., mood disorders such as anxiety and depression, social skills impairment in ADHD) have begun to be used in ASD treatment. For example, cognitive-behavioral interventions targeting anxiety (e.g., relaxation, thought stopping), depression (e.g., coping statements), and social skill impairments (e.g., social scripts) are being used with individuals who have ASD without concomitant mental retardation (see Klinger & Williams, 2009, for a review). More research is needed to demonstrate the efficacy of these techniques for individuals with ASD. There also are approaches that have been applied in interventions with individuals with ASD that have not yet been studied using basic scientific standards; thus, to date there is no evidence that they work but there also is no evidence that they either do not work or are harmful. These practices may be found to work with specific individuals, but it is best to not use them in isolation from evidence-based interventions that are known to work. In addition, there are interventions that clearly demonstrate a lack of efficacy that pose significant health risks or are otherwise considered harmful, and these should be avoided. For further exploration of this topic, readers are directed to a number of reviews (Chorpita et al., 2002; Green, 1996b; Herbert et al., 2002; Myers et al., 2007; New York State Department of Health, 1999; Rogers, 1998, 1999; Rogers & Vismara, 2008; Smith, 1996; Smith et al., 2007).

In sum, it is vital that evidence-based practices be utilized whenever possible in order to effect the best and most rapid change for individuals with ASD. Great strides have been made in identifying aspects of interventions that have a solid evidence base, and providers and caregivers are encouraged to make use of the national reports that will be generated in the coming years. However, it will continue to be important for policy makers, educators, parents, and providers to support the scientific evaluation of interventions so that resources may be channeled into the most effective methods of intervention (Kasari, 2002).

Questions to Consider

When Should Intervention Begin?

General developmental intervention should begin as soon as a concern regarding a child's development has been identified. This may occur through state agencies providing interventions for very young children identified as at risk or exhibiting delay in any area of development. Beyond general developmental interventions, experts recommend that ASD-specific intervention begin as soon as a diagnosis on the autism spectrum is seriously considered. Due to limited diagnostic resources, waiting lists at diagnostic clinics often are long, and valuable intervention time is wasted while a child and family await a formal diagnosis. If the child has an ASD, beginning ASD-specific intervention during these valuable learning years will lead to better progress. If the child does not have an ASD, treatment with ASD-specific interventions will not be harmful (Dawson, Ashman, & Carver, 2000).

Many of the earliest symptoms of ASD include a lack of age-appropriate social communication skills such as imitation, shared or joint attention, and turn taking. These delays have been related to later difficulties in language development, play skills, and social relationships. When intervention is started at a younger age, outcome is significantly better (Handleman & Harris, 2000; National Research Council, 2001). Research indicates that the earliest years of life are marked by incredible rates of learning and appear to be a "sensitive period" for maximizing impact of early interventions (see Dawson et al., 2000, for a review). With early and specific intervention that is intensive (i.e., at least 25 hours a week), 75% to 95% of children with ASD learn to talk and 50% of children with ASD succeed in a regular education kindergarten classroom with little support (Lord, Risi, & Pickles, 2004; Smith et al., 2007; Wetherby & Woods, 2006). Early intervention that is appropriately designed and implemented may save up to a million dollars in lifetime care for each individual with ASD (Jacobson, Mulick, & Green, 1998). However, appropriate intervention at any point in an individual's life can create significant behavior change and may lead to greater independence later in life.

Who Should Intervene?

Unfortunately, there is a deficit of both early interventionists and special educators available, especially those trained to work with low-incidence disabilities such as ASD. A critical element in ensuring progress for children with ASD is for all interventionists to have training in the characteristics of ASD and also in evidence-based techniques, specifically in those practices that have the greatest evidence of efficacy. All professional staff and providers from different disciplines working with students and individuals with ASD need to understand the rationale behind ASD-specific interventions so they may not only apply these correctly (i.e., to fidelity; see below) but also may monitor, evaluate, and modify the approach as they are working with a particular student (Jones, 2006). It is important to note that most research involves training less "qualified" providers or trainees to apply the treatment being researched; however, these interventionists are trained to *fidelity* on the practice being implemented, that is, they are trained to ensure that the intervention is being implemented as intended. This has implications for school systems; frequently schools use paraprofessionals to address the individual needs of children with ASD but typically do not have the resources to train these providers specifically and fail to delineate their roles clearly (Myers et al., 2007). Regardless of their position, school personnel who do not have appropriate training in ASD-specific interventions and techniques may not value the intervention or may administer the technique poorly and stop using it because they perceive that it does not work (Tincani, 2007).

Recent research suggests that teaching parents to work with very young children with ASD in their natural environment and to embed ASD-specific interventions in their day-to-day routines works very well to increase social communication (McConachie & Diggle, 2007; Wetherby & Woods, 2006). Parent-implemented intervention is on the NPDC list of practices with confirmed evidence base for individuals with ASD. Empowering parents as active partners in their child's treatment is vital to both the child's progress and the health and well-being of the family. Parental involvement in a child's interventions may tend to decrease as the child moves into the school system, and a child with ASD is unlikely to transfer skills learned at school to use in the home setting without targeted effort by his or her family.

The National Research Council (2001) recommended initial training sessions as well as ongoing consultation with both parents and interventionists. Specifically, it is recommended that

> at a minimum, teachers should have some special preparation (e.g., pre-service course work, equivalent in-service training, workshops, and supervised practice in research-based practices in ASD) and should have well-trained, experienced support personnel available to provide ongoing training and additional consultation. (National Research Council, 2001, p. 224)

Many of the strategies on the NPDC list are behavioral strategies (e.g., prompting, time delay, and chaining), which take time and supervised practice in order to learn to implement appropriately.

Where Should the Intervention Take Place?

It is recommended that interventions for young children with ASD balance individual (one-on-one) skill-building therapy, which is typically either home- or center-based, with small-group therapy, which usually occurs in a classroom setting. This balance of services may vary depending on the skills of the child and on the extent and nature of previous interventions. For example, although some young children may be ready to enter a small preschool classroom with peers with typical development and learn in that environment, others may require intensive one-on-one intervention before they would be ready to receive the benefits of inclusive intervention.

There is much discussion in educational groups regarding inclusion of individuals with ASD in regular education settings. Inclusion for individuals with ASD has been associated with better outcomes in terms of social development and academics, although results of the existing research are mixed (Harrower & Dunlap, 2001; Schreibman, 2005). The available evidence regarding interventions targeting increased and improved social interactions for individuals with ASD makes it clear that inclusion and integration with their peers with typical development, as well as peer-mediated instruction, is warranted to promote treatment effects, but there are some qualifiers for this statement (Bellini, Peters, Benner, & Hopf, 2007; McConnell, 2002; Tuchman-Ginsburg & Shaw, 2008). Specifically:

- It is not helpful to include a child with ASD fully unless the child already has good skills for interacting appropriately with adults and other children (Myles, Simpson, Ormsbee, & Erickson, 1993).
- It is important that the child's peers also be socially competent (McConnell, 2002).
- Successful inclusion is related to the level of expertise of the student's entire educational team.
- Without proper training and understanding of ASD in the classroom, a student's symptoms of ASD may limit the educational experience for the included child as well as the rest of the class (Goodman & Williams, 2007).

Harrower and Dunlap (2001) identified that inclusion may be facilitated by the use of antecedent procedures (e.g., picture schedules), delayed contingencies to promote generalization (e.g., delaying reward for on-task behaviors in lieu of constant supervision), self-management strategies (e.g., self-monitoring or management), and peer-mediated interventions (e.g., peer tutoring). Overall, it may be concluded that "inclusion is a necessary, but not likely sufficient, condition for social interaction interventions" with children with ASD (McConnell, 2002, p. 367).

As noted above, generalizing skills learned in one environment to other environments is exceedingly important and difficult for individuals with ASD; thus, implementation of interventions in natural settings, such as by parents in the home setting, is vital. It is important that a structured and supportive environment that is understandable to the child be maintained across settings. Transitions between settings must be effectively planned for, supported, and managed.

What Should Be Taught?

Although there is an extensive list of various areas in which to intervene with children with ASD, what is taught at any age should include all aspects of development in which the child is not progressing as expected. Evidence indicates that language acquisition is predictive of better outcome of individuals with ASD; thus, a strong focus in the youngest ages should be on developing a spontaneous, functional communication system with an effort to stimulate verbal, nonverbal/gestural, and affective modalities. In addition, the significant social growth seen during typical development in the first 5 years of life points to the developmental necessity of explicitly teaching social skills to children with ASD. Children with ASD are not well attuned to their social environments and therefore are not attending to, imitating, or motivated by attention from their parents or peers. Teaching these core skills explicitly and in a developmentally appropriate manner is important to build a solid foundation of social skills so that more complex and later developing skills can be taught as the child ages and progresses. As with any child, it also is important to attend to the cognitive, motor, and adaptive/self-help skills that are delayed in development. Teaching of organizational and other classroom skills typically is necessary for success in a classroom or other group setting.

An additional important consideration in determining where to serve the child with autism is the many transitions between service systems. These are important events requiring advanced planning and careful consideration each year, but particularly during the transition between preschool and kindergarten and from school attendance to adulthood and services outside the school system (Forest, Horner, Lewis-Palmer, & Todd, 2004; Volkmar et al., 1999). IDEA (2006) requires transition planning by 16 years of age. Legally, however, if a child requires transition planning at an earlier age or as part of the Individualized Education Program (IEP) development, the process should be initiated when it is appropriate for the child. Overall, the transition plan should represent "a shift from academic to vocational services and from remediating deficits to fostering abilities" (Myers et al., 2007, p. 1167). Decisions regarding postsecondary placement and vocational paths are made during this time, and it is recommended that plans for transition and beyond include a component of ongoing skill development and education in independent living skills. NCLB (2001) requires that in addition to academic development, students also must be ensured equality of opportunity, full participation, independent living, and economic self-sufficiency.

Any disruptive behavior will be addressed best in context (i.e., in the setting or settings in which the behavior occurs), utilizing a functional approach and focusing on developing missing skills as well as replacement behaviors (e.g., using differential reinforcement of alternative and more acceptable behaviors). Behavioral strategies focused on positive behavior support, with the goal of increasing appropriate behaviors, are recommended over strategies focused on punishment and decreasing unwanted behaviors (Horner, Carr, Strain, Todd, & Reed, 2002). Disruptive and problematic behaviors addressed with behavioral interventions (e.g., stimulus- and instruction-based procedures, extinction, reinforcement) are noted to be as high as 80% to 90% effective. However, it should be noted that the use of functional assessment tools is a strong predictor of successful behavioral intervention (Horner et al., 2002), and this step is too often omitted in behavioral planning. Additional factors of importance are that behavioral procedures be implemented by families and teachers and through a structural change in the environment, such as a change in organization or the behavior of others in the individual's environment (e.g., stimulus control or environmental modification). It is recommended that behavioral support of school-aged children with ASD include the following considerations: "minimize presentation of aversive events, maximize contingent access to rewarding activities and outcomes, and minimize the likelihood that problem behavior will be rewarded" (Horner et al., 2002, p. 435).

How Should We Intervene?

Among the critical elements in intervening with children with ASD, there is a clear emphasis on intensity of intervention. Research clearly has demonstrated that at least 25 hours a week of active engagement in planned programming is required for promoting the best outcome in children with ASD. Active engagement is defined as the child working toward individualized goals in an effortful manner. Further, there is evidence that children with ASD have difficulty maintaining gains, which provides support for needing children with ASD to be engaged in active learning all 52 weeks of the year.

Children need to be engaged in activities that are specifically designed to target their individualized objectives and that use good teaching strategies. The developmental appropriateness of both the teaching techniques and the targeted objectives must be considered, as progress will be optimized by following a developmental sequence. The use of systematic, planned, and developmentally appropriate instruction is critical. According to special education law, individualized objectives should be observable, measurable behaviors and skills, and ongoing measurement of progress toward objectives must be documented frequently (i.e., at least every 3 months) so that changes in the intervention program may be made if progress is not forthcoming.

It is important that providers, early intervention agencies, school districts, and parents work together to identify programming that is matched to the individual child's needs, developed and implemented to promote educational gains, and not limited only to current program availability (Iovannone, Dunlap, Huber, & Kincaid, 2003; Mandlawitz, 2002). In the early years (birth to 3 years of age), the Individualized Family Service Plan (IFSP) guides each child's services, while the IEP is the written plan for the school-aged (ages 3 to 21 years) individual's education. In either case, these documents for students with ASD require an understanding of the diagnosis that allows school professionals to "move beyond the standard, procedural approach to IEPs and to make the process a dynamic one" (Smith, Slattery, & Knopp, 1993, p. 2).

In terms of specific techniques, readers are referred to the list of evidence-based practices provided by the NPDC (Tuchman-Ginsburg & Shaw, 2008) reviewed previously in this section, and to future versions of this list as the evidence base expands. Given the availability of objective reviews (e.g., the National Autism Center's National Standards Project and the NPDC reviews) and the current level of focus on identifying and disseminating effective interventions, it will be important for providers, teachers, and caregivers to ensure that techniques being used with individuals with ASD are both based in adequate evidence and actually are being implemented correctly.

Some interventions, such as those based in applied behavior analysis (ABA), target specific skill deficits for remediation, while others are designed to teach the person with ASD to compensate for his or her deficits in a particular area, and still others are used to alter the environment in order to better support the person with autism. The strategies presented here represent examples of either approach to intervention.

Approaches that rely on principles of applied behavior analysis are designed to remediate deficits. Many of these approaches have been found to be effective and are considered evidence-based by multiple groups. ABA is a term used to refer to techniques involving the application of known principles of learning with a goal of altering socially important human behaviors. ABA is not synonymous with a particular package or program despite the term frequently being used in that manner and despite the fact that Lovaas' (Lovaas, 1987; McEachin et al., 1993) application of these techniques is the most widely researched comprehensive program for treating young children with autism and has the strongest evidence base. A variety of different programs use principles of ABA to address skill building in individuals with ASD. These programs include interventions that are highly structured and adult-driven (e.g., Lovaas, UCLA Young Autism Project) and those that are more based in the natural environment and child-driven (e.g., Pivotal Response Treatments; Koegel & Koegel, 2006). Some behavioral strategies applied with individuals with ASD include:

- *prompting*—temporary assistance or antecedent implemented to increase the likelihood of correct response;
- *time delay*—allowing short delay before providing a prompt;
- *reinforcement*—stimulus or event that follows a behavior and makes it more likely to occur in the future;
- *task analysis*—breaking a complex behavior down into smaller component parts;
- *chaining*—learning a complex behavior by first learning each component part and linking these together;
- *differential reinforcement*—providing reinforcement for desired behaviors while removing reinforcement for undesired behaviors;
- *discrete trial training*—behaviorally based instruction routine that cycles through the antecedent-behavior-consequence sequence;
- *extinction*—removing a reinforcer for behavior to decrease the likelihood of it occurring in the future;
- *functional behavior assessment*—collecting data to determine antecedents and consequences of a specific behavior;
- *response interruption/redirection*—interrupting an undesired behavior and prompting a desired behavior; and

- *stimulus control*—correlation between the antecedent and the subsequent response and teaching which antecedents are most important.

Given that it is clear that these strategies work well with children with autism, extensive training in this area is recommended for professionals.

One area that must be targeted in ASD is the area of social skills, as this is a core deficit. Social skills training utilizes behavioral and other strategies such as pivotal response training, adult prompting, social skills groups, social stories, video modeling, peer-mediated instruction, and environmental modifications (Bellini et al., 2007; Matson, Matson, & Rivet, 2007; Rogers, 2000). Video modeling has been used increasingly to improve social-communication skills (e.g., conversation and play skills), functional skills (e.g., self-help or purchasing skills), perspective-taking skills, and behavioral functioning (e.g., prosocial behaviors and on-task behavior; Bellini & Akullian, 2007; Delano, 2007). On the whole, the most effective strategies for teaching social skills appear to be those based on an understanding of specific characteristics of ASD, specifically tailored to the students' individual strengths and weaknesses, and applied frequently to facilitate and maintain treatment effects (Matson et al., 2007; Rogers, 2000; White, Keonig, & Scahill, 2007). These interventions may be conducted on an individual or group level, and in the home, school, or clinical environments; however, studies suggest a need for these interventions to occur in the natural social environment to promote generalization and maintenance effectively (Bellini et al., 2007).

In addition to considering techniques to remediate the deficits in autism, it also is important to consider teaching methods to compensate for deficits, especially in higher functioning students with ASD. The use of social narratives, such as the Social Stories™ technique developed by Carol Gray, has grown in popularity in school and clinical settings for higher functioning individuals with ASD. These may be used to discuss following routines, academic activities, social situations, and other situations encountered by individuals with ASD (Gray & Garand, 1993), and are designed to teach the person with ASD to think through social and other affective situations that he or she does not understand intuitively. A Social Story™ consists of a short narrative detailing a specific social situation by breaking it down into understandable components. This narrative is presented in first-person perspective and is intended to help the reader better understand the expectations and appropriate behaviors associated with a given social situation. Self-management strategies also may be taught so that the person with ASD can organize his or her own supports and rewards for desirable behaviors.

Although much progress has been made in remediating the core deficits of ASD, current evidence indicates that these deficits will be lifelong. Further, most people with ASD will require environmental alterations at some point in their lives to support their learning and behavior. Visual supports and structured work systems are examples of these types of modifications to the environment. Perhaps the most widely used program of visual strategies is from the TEACCH (Treatment and Education of Autistic and related Communication-handicapped Children) method of "structured teaching," which involves modification of the environment, visual supports, and the implementation of structured activities and routines to build skills (Dettmer, Simpson, Myles, & Ganz, 2000; Myers et al., 2007).

Developing a Comprehensive Intervention Package

Arguments over specific brand-name programs often overshadow the evidence in favor of critical elements and evidence-based practices of intervention. An objective consumer of the available research is encouraged to consider that the ideal intervention program may require an age- and developmentally appropriate integration of a range of approaches and techniques that have received the best empirical support thus far. Practices that encourage the development of relationships with both the adults and the peers in the person's environment—those that remediate the core deficits, those that teach the individual to compensate for his or her weaknesses, and those that support or accommodate the person with ASD—all may be necessary in order to achieve his or her maximum potential and to function most adaptively. Although combining practices is suggested, it is important to understand that evidence-based practices are known to be effective only when they are implemented as they were tested, thus fidelity to the practice must be high. Furthermore, although these techniques are recommended specifically for children with ASD, such interventions would likely have a positive impact on all children served by these programs and their providers, leading to a net gain in overall quality and outcome.

Considerations for Interventions With Adults With ASD

Although this publication is focused on children, it is essential to note the lifelong presence and impact of this disorder, and a brief review of difficulties seen in adults with ASD and relevant interventions is warranted. Furthermore, all interventions with children and adolescents with ASD must be planned and conducted with adulthood in mind; thus, a review of skills that often require continued intervention in adulthood may guide more targeted interventions in earlier stages of development.

By age 21, young adults with ASD are no longer served by the public school system. With a growing number of individuals being diagnosed with ASD and as the increasingly positive long-term outcomes following early and sustained intervention are observed, there is a dire need for affordable transition and support services that span all possible outcomes for individuals with ASD. Furthermore, with a trend of moving away from institutional facilities toward inclusion and community treatment of developmental disorders, support for individuals with ASD will range from supported employment to college programs. As individuals with ASD continue to age, there will be an increased need for geriatric services and placements that can meet the unique needs of older adults with ASD. Doka and Lavin (2003) noted that as adults with ASD and other developmental disabilities age, there is an increased need for services but a decreased number of service providers that can meet their needs.

The social, communication, and behavioral symptoms of ASD have the potential to impede adults with ASD in being successful. Adults with ASD often benefit from continued intervention and social skills training to assist in successful social interaction and community living. Due to pervasive social difficulties, adults with ASD can be perceived as harassing, insensitive, or even dangerous, making it difficult to sustain employment or complete postsecondary degrees. Many adults with ASD require continued treatment to build social and communication skills and to troubleshoot misunderstandings that occur in their environments.

As a guide for planning interventions to benefit adults with ASD, Holtz, Owings, and Ziegert (2006) identified the following workplace-specific social and communication skills warranting intervention. These skills may be addressed throughout a child's education:

- listening skills,
- recognizing when help is needed and obtaining help when necessary,
- level of response to others,
- eye contact during regular interaction,
- general manners such as responding to greetings and not interrupting others,
- awareness of others' personal space,
- understanding the difference between private and public behaviors,
- flexibility to handle changes in schedule or environment, and
- understanding of appropriate and inappropriate conversation topics and behaviors.

Given the wide range of outcomes for adults with ASD, no one treatment approach or intervention is appropriate, nor is there sufficient empirical evidence to demonstrate that a single approach is most effective. However, the following recommendations are most supported by the literature (Dillion, 2007; Holmes, 1990; Holtz et al., 2006; Jabarin, Crocombe, Gralton, & Carter, 2001; Van Bourgondien, Reichle, & Schopler, 2003):

- a coordinated system of intervention and support that addresses academic transition, job training and coaching, college support, daily living skills, communication, and social skills;
- training for service providers on empirically validated supports and behavioral strategies;
- collaborative approach among the individual, parent, mentor, and support agencies with an emphasis on developing maximum independence as appropriate to each individual's developmental and cognitive level; and
- emphasis on self-advocacy.

Issues regarding aging and late adulthood for individuals with ASD are beginning to receive additional attention. In 2004, there were estimated to be more than 525,000 individuals over the age of 60 with developmental disabilities such as autism, and this number is expected to double by the year 2030 (Heller, Factor, & Hahn, 1999). With the introduction of early diagnosis and intervention, greater numbers of adults with ASD are employed and thus eligible for retirement. The needs of adults with ASD are varied, but may include access to healthcare, retirement counseling, long-term care in a nursing home, and/or independent living support as their caregivers die. The emerging geriatric population with ASD will warrant special attention in future years.

Family Support

Even after families adjust to the initial diagnosis of a child with ASD, the lifelong and chronic nature of the disorder typically causes ongoing stress and requires frequent coping in families. A number of studies have demonstrated that having a child or sibling diagnosed with ASD can be a more significant stressor than having a child or sibling with typical development, chronic or life-threatening illness, or another developmental disability (Bagenholm & Gillberg, 1991; Bouma & Schweitzer, 1990; Rodrigue, Geffken, & Morgan, 1993; Verté, Roeyers, & Buysse, 2003; Wolf, Fisman, Ellison, & Freeman, 1998). Among families with one or more children diagnosed with an ASD, which often leads to increased physical and emotional stress, parents may tend to take out their frustrations on each other, potentially resulting in divorce, separation, or other marital difficulties (Lavin, 2001). Family members may feel increased pressure to serve as a primary caregiver for the child or sibling with ASD (Bouma & Schweitzer, 1990). In fact, the amount of stress a family feels in response to increased caregiving burdens may be proportional to the number of members in a family, such that single mothers who shoulder the caregiving burden alone experience significantly more stress than large families with multiple caregivers who can share responsibility (Bouma & Schweitzer, 1990). The American Academy of Pediatrics (Myers et al., 2007) suggested that it is important to help parents find effective respite caregivers so that they can have an occasional break or night off. This may help preserve the emotional health of the family members and remove some of the associated stress from the increased caregiving burden.

In addition to increased caregiving stress, having a family member with ASD often leads to increased financial stress. For example, Gray (2002) reported that even 10 years after the initial diagnosis, mothers of children with ASD often were unable to work full-time, as they were required to continue primary caregiving responsibilities. This decrease in maternal income coupled with the expense of continued therapy and intervention services often leads to increased financial stress within the family system. To help family members cope with the financial burden of caring for a child with ASD, it is recommended that professionals inform parents about Medicaid, in-home and community-based waiver services, Supplemental Security Income benefits, and other financial subsidies (Myers et al., 2007). However, professionals themselves often lack this type of comprehensive knowledge about these statewide and federal services.

The National Research Council's Committee on Educational Interventions for Children with Autism (2001) recommended that professionals providing intervention to children with ASD consider the family as valued members of the treatment team and should make an effort to include them in decision-making and caregiving decisions. Education about autism and training in behavioral skills has been demonstrated to help parents feel more effective with their children with autism and to reduce stress, anxiety, and family dysfunction (Tonge et al., 2006). The American Academy of Pediatrics (Myers et al., 2007) outlined several ways in which professionals can help include family members in the treatment process:

- educate them about ASD and the treatments used,
- give them training necessary to provide intervention to their child with ASD,
- help them to navigate the medical/psychological system,
- provide ASD resources and support group information,
- give them the information to effectively advocate for their child's needs (e.g., information about early intervention or IEPs), and
- recommend or refer them for individual or family therapy when appropriate.

In addition to supporting parents of children with ASD, there is a growing awareness that siblings also need support. There is a need for emotional support for siblings of a person with ASD, and siblings often share some of the language and social difficulties experienced by the family member with ASD. Because of the genetic nature of this disorder, it is common for siblings to display the "Broad Autism Phenotype" (Losh & Piven, 2007) in which some symptoms, but not the entire disorder, are present. There is little methodologically sound research on interventions and/or support groups for siblings of a child with ASD. A few studies have been conducted that examined the effectiveness of sibling support groups. Overall, parents and the participating siblings generally rate support groups favorably and indicate that there are some benefits for the participating siblings (Marcus, Kunce, & Schopler, 2005; Smith & Perry, 2005).

Conclusions

The screening, diagnosis, and treatment of individuals with ASD are constantly evolving based on advances in ongoing research and clinical practice. Overall, however, the current review of research reveals several significant and guiding principles for the field, as listed below.

- Early screening for developmental delays, including ASD, is essential in promoting long-term positive outcomes for young children with and without ASD. Furthermore, research indicates that screening for ASD is quite reliable at very young ages, and such findings require measures be taken to utilize this advance fully.
- Interdisciplinary diagnostic evaluations that consider developmental history, behavioral symptoms of autism, language development, and cognitive functioning are important in differentiating between ASD and other developmental disorders. When ASD-specific instruments are employed, an increasingly accurate diagnosis of individuals with symptoms of ASD is obtained. Using these measures is essential to the planning of psychosocial and educational interventions.

- Although the treatment literature is limited at this time, it also is dynamic and there is promise of identifying a number of "key ingredients" related to improved prognosis across areas of functioning for individuals with ASD and their families. There are a number of treatment strategies with basis in evidence, and these bases are becoming more solid over time. Service providers, educators, and caregivers are encouraged not only to be aware of appropriate interventions, but also to strive to implement identified interventions to fidelity.

Readers are encouraged to remain cautious but hopeful in their pursuits of all three areas discussed in this volume. Make use of the existing resources and demand solid, evidence-based practice in these pursuits. Keep abreast of the ever-changing literature and conceptualization of ASD, and apply these findings to each individual with a family based, culturally sensitive approach.

Resources

American Academy of Pediatrics Identification and Evaluation of Children with Autism Spectrum Disorders Policy
http://www.aap.org/healthtopics/autism.cfm
This site features the American Academy of Pediatrics' policy regarding identification and evaluation of children with ASD, found under Professional Resources.

Modified Checklist for Autism in Toddlers (M-CHAT)
http://www.firstsigns.org/downloads/m-chat.pdf
This site has the M-CHAT available for download and professional use.

Communication and Symbolic Behavior Scales Infant-Toddler Checklist (CSBS ITC)
http://firstwords.fsu.edu/pdf/checklist.pdf
This site has the CSBS ITC available for download and professional use.

Diagnosis Web Sites

University of Michigan Autism & Communication Disorders Center
http://www.umaccweb.com
This site provides information regarding the Autism Diagnostic Observation Schedule (ADOS) and the Autism Diagnostic Interview-Revised (ADI-R).

Western Psychological Services
http://www.wpspublish.com
This site features Autism Diagnostic Observation Schedule (ADOS) training information and allows visitors to purchase the ADOS or the Autism Diagnostic Interview-Revised (ADI-R).

Treatment/Intervention Web Sites

American Academy of Pediatrics Management of Children With Autism Spectrum Disorders Policy
http://www.aap.org/healthtopics/autism.cfm
This site features the American Academy of Pediatrics' policy regarding treatment and interventions with children with ASD, found under Professional Resources.

National Autism Center
http://www.nationalautismcenter.org
This site contains information regarding best practices for working with children and adolescents with ASD, including information from a National Standards Project report to promote use of best-practice intervention strategies.

The National Professional Development Center on Autism Spectrum Disorders
http://www.fpg.unc.edu/~autismPDC
This site provides reviews and reports regarding evidence-based interventions and how to implement identified interventions appropriately.

Autism Internet Modules
http://www.autisminternetmodules.org
This site offers Web-based training providing information, multimedia demonstrations, case examples, and critical thinking exercises regarding evidence-based practices for caregivers and professionals working with individuals with ASD.

Professional Training Resource Library
http://depts.washington.edu/isei/ptrl/PTRL_Purpose.php
Offered in partnership with the Association of University Centers on Disabilities (AUCD), this site provides a range of free materials to support professional training in the area of early intervention.

TEACCH
http://www.teacch.com
This is the site for the Treatment and Education of Autistic and related Communication-handicapped Children located in North Carolina. It provides online information resources for families, educators, and professionals regarding intervention strategies across the lifespan.

Sibling Support Project
http://www.siblingsupport.org
This site contains information about the Sibling Support Project and associated listservs, resources for child and adult siblings of individuals with special needs and for families regarding sibling support issues, and Sibshop programming.

Planning for Adulthood Web Sites

Life Journey Through Autism:
A Guide for Transition to Adulthood

http://www.researchautism.org/resources/reading/documents/
TransitionGuide.pdf

This site offers a downloadable guide written by Holtz, Owings, and Ziegert for the Organization for Autism Research and the Southwest Autism Research & Resource Center.

The College Program for Children With Asperger's Syndrome at Marshall University

http://www.marshall.edu/coe/atc/modelcollege.htm

This site describes a program using positive behavior support to help students with ASD succeed in college.

The University of Alabama Autism Spectrum Disorders College Transition and Support Program

http://www.autism-clinic.ua.edu

This site describes a program providing individualized academic and social transition and support services for students with ASD at The University of Alabama.

General ASD Information and Advocacy Web Sites

Autism Society of America

http://www.autism-society.org

This is the site for a grassroots organization providing resources, advocacy, and support for individuals with ASD and their families.

Autism Speaks

http://www.autismspeaks.org

This is the site for a nonprofit organization providing research funding and resources for families and professionals regarding ASD.

Centers for Disease Control and Prevention Autism Information Center

http://www.cdc.gov/ncbddd/autism

This site is a comprehensive source of information regarding symptoms, screening and diagnosis, and treatment and therapy for practitioners, parents, and researchers.

References

American Psychiatric Association. (2000). *Diagnostic and statistical manual of mental disorders* (4th ed., text revision). Washington, DC: Author.

Bagenholm, A., & Gillberg, C. (1991). Psychosocial effects on siblings of children with autism and mental retardation: A population-based study. *Journal of Mental Deficiency Research, 35,* 291–307.

Baranek, G. T. (1999). Autism during infancy: A retrospective video analysis of sensory-motor and social behaviors at 9–12 months of age. *Journal of Autism and Developmental Disorders, 29,* 213–224.

Bellini, S., & Akullian, J. (2007). A meta-analysis of video modeling and video self-modeling interventions for children and adolescents with autism spectrum disorders. *Exceptional Children, 73,* 264–287.

Bellini, S., Peters, J. K., Benner, L., & Hopf, A. (2007). A meta-analysis of school-based social skills interventions for children with autism spectrum disorders. *Remedial and Special Education, 28,* 153–162.

Berument, S. K., Rutter, M., Lord, C., Pickles, A., & Bailey, A. (1999). Autism Screening Questionnaire: Diagnostic validity. *British Journal of Psychiatry, 175,* 444–451.

Bouma, R., & Schweitzer, R. (1990). The impact of chronic illness on family stress: A comparison between autism and cystic fibrosis. *Journal of Clinical Psychology, 46,* 722–730.

Brian, J., Bryson, S. E., Garon, N., Roberts, W., Smith, I. M., Szatmari, P., et al. (2008). Clinical assessment of autism in high-risk 18-month-olds. *Autism, 12,* 433–456.

Bricker, D., Squires, J., & Mounts, L. (1995). *Ages and Stages Questionnaire: A parent-completed, child-monitoring system.* Baltimore: Brookes.

Bryson, S. E., McDermott, C., Rombough, V., Brian, J., & Zwaigenbaum, L. (2008). The Autism Observation Scale for Infants (AOSI): Scale development and reliability data. *Journal of Autism and Developmental Disorders, 38,* 731–738.

Centers for Disease Control and Prevention. (2007). Prevalence of Autism Spectrum Disorders—Autism and Developmental Disabilities Monitoring Network, six sites, United States, 2002. *MMWR, 56,* SS-1.

Chakrabarti, S., & Fombonne, E. (2005). Pervasive developmental disorder in preschool children: Confirmation of high prevalence. *American Journal of Psychiatry, 162,* 1133–1141.

Chorpita, B., Yim, L., Donkervoet, J., Arensdorf, A., Amundsen, M. J., McGee, C., et al. (2002). Toward large-scale implementation of empirically supported treatments for children: A review and observations by the Hawaii Empirical Basis to Services Task Force. *Clinical Psychology: Science and Practice, 9,* 165–190.

Constantino, J. N., Davis, S. A., Todd, R. D., Schindler, M. K., Gross, M. M., Brophy, S. L., et al. (2003). Validation of a brief quantitative genetic measure of autistic traits: Comparison of the Social Responsiveness Scale with the Autism Diagnostic Interview-Revised. *Journal of Autism and Developmental Disorders, 25,* 427–433.

Constantino, J. N., & Gruber, C. P. (2005). *Social Responsiveness Scale*. Los Angeles: Western Psychological Services.

Dawson, G., Ashman, S. B., & Carver, L. J. (2000). The role of early experience in shaping behavioral and brain development and its implications for social policy. *Development and Psychopathology, 12,* 695–712.

Dawson, G., & Osterling, J. (1997). Early intervention in autism: Effectiveness and common elements of current approaches. In M. Guralnick (Ed.), *The effectiveness of early intervention* (pp. 307–326). Baltimore: Brookes.

Delano, M. E. (2007). Video modeling interventions for individuals with autism. *Remedial and Special Education, 28,* 33–42.

Dettmer, S., Simpson, R. L., Myles, B., & Ganz, J. B. (2000). The use of visual supports to facilitate transitions of students with autism. *Focus on Autism and Other Developmental Disabilities, 15,* 163–169.

Dillion, M. (2007). Creating supports for college students with Asperger syndrome through collaboration. *College Student Journal, 41,* 499–504.

Doka, K., & Lavin, C. (2003). The paradox of aging with developmental disability: Increasing needs, declining resources. *Aging International, 28,* 135–154.

Dumont-Mathieu, T., & Fein, D. (2005). Screening for autism in young children: The Modified Checklist for Autism in Toddlers (M-CHAT) and other measures. *Mental Retardation and Developmental Disabilities Research Review, 11,* 253–262.

Fenske, E., Zalenski, S., Krantz, P., & McClannahan, L. (1985). Age at intervention and treatment outcome for autistic children in a comprehensive intervention program. *Analysis and Interventions for Developmental Disabilities, 5,* 49–58.

Filipek, P., Accardo, P., Baranek, G., Cook, E., Dawson, G., Gordon, B., et al. (1999). The screening and diagnosis of autism spectrum disorders. *Journal of Autism and Developmental Disorders, 29,* 439–475.

Filipek, P. A., Accardo, P. J., Ashwal, S., Baranek, G. T., Cook., E. H., Dawson, G., et al. (2000). Practice parameter: Screening and diagnosis of autism: Report of the Quality Standards Subcommittee of the American Academy of Neurology and the Child Neurology Society. *Neurology, 55,* 468–479.

Fombonne, E. (2005). Epidemiological studies of pervasive developmental disorders. In F. R Volkmar, R. Paul, A. Klin, & D. Cohen (Eds.), *Handbook of autism and pervasive developmental disorders, Vol. 1: Diagnosis, development, neurobiology, and behavior* (3rd ed., pp. 42–69). Hoboken, NJ: Wiley.

Forest, E. J., Horner, R. H., Lewis-Palmer, T., & Todd, A. W. (2004). Transitions for young children with autism from preschool to kindergarten. *Journal of Positive Behavior Interventions, 6,* 103–112.

Goin-Kochel, R. P., & Mackintosh, V. H. (2007). Parental report on the use of treatments and therapies for children with autism spectrum disorders. *Research in Autism Spectrum Disorders, 1,* 195–209.

Goldstein, H. (2002). Communication intervention for children with autism: A review of treatment efficacy. *Journal of Autism and Developmental Disorders, 32,* 373–396.

Goodman, G., & Williams, C. M. (2007). Interventions for increasing the academic engagement of students with autism spectrum disorders in inclusive classrooms. *Teaching Exceptional Children, 39,* 53–61.

Gotham, K., Risi, S., Dawson, G., Tager-Flusberg, H., Joseph, R., Carter, A., et al. (2008). A replication of the Autism Diagnostic Observation Schedule (ADOS) revised algorithms. *Journal of the American Academy of Child and Adolescent Psychiatry, 47,* 642–651.

Gray, C., & Garand, J. D. (1993). Social stories: Improving responses of students with autism with accurate social information. *Focus on Autistic Behavior, 8,* 1–10.

Gray, D. E. (2002). Ten years on: A longitudinal study of families of children with autism. *Journal of Intellectual and Developmental Disability, 27,* 215–222.

Green, D. (2001). Autism and "voodoo science" treatments. *Priorities for Health, 13,* 27–32, 69.

Green, G. (1996a). Evaluating claims about treatments for autism. In C. Maurice, G. Green, & S. C. Luce (Eds.), *Behavioral intervention for young children with autism: A manual for parents and professionals* (pp. 15–28). Austin, TX: Pro-Ed.

Green, G. (1996b). Early behavioral intervention for autism: What does research tell us? In C. Maurice, G. Green, & S. C. Luce (Eds.), *Behavioral intervention for young children with autism: A manual for parents and professionals* (pp. 29–44). Austin, TX: Pro-Ed.

Handleman, J. S., & Harris, S. L. (2000). *Preschool education programs for children with autism* (2nd ed.). Austin, TX: Pro-Ed.

Harris, S., & Handleman, J. (2000). Age and IQ at intake as predictors of placement for young children: A four- to six-year follow-up. *Journal of Autism and Developmental Disorders, 30,* 137–142.

Harrower, J. K., & Dunlap, G. (2001). Including children with autism in general education classrooms: A review of effective strategies. *Behavior Modification, 25,* 762–784.

Heller, T., Factor, A., & Hahn, J. (1999). Residential transitions from nursing homes for adults with cerebral palsy. *Disability and Rehabilitation, 21,* 277–283.

Herbert, J., & Sharp, I. (2001). Pseudoscientific treatments for autism. *Priorities for Health, 13,* 23–26, 59.

Herbert, J., Sharp, I., & Gaudiano, B. (2002). Separating fact from fiction in the etiology and treatment of autism: A scientific review of the evidence. *The Scientific Review of Mental Health Practice, 1*(1). Retrieved February 20, 2009, from http://www.srmhp.org/0101/autism.html

Hix-Small, H., Marks, K., Squires, J., & Nickel, R. (2007). Impact of implementing developmental screening at 12 and 24 months in a pediatric practice. *Pediatrics, 120,* 381–389.

Holmes, D. L. (1990). Community-based services for children and adults with autism: The Eden Family of Programs. *Journal of Autism and Developmental Disorders, 20,* 339–351.

Holtz, K., Owings, N., & Ziegert, A. (2006). *Life journey through autism: A guide for transition to adulthood.* Retrieved from http://

www.researchautism.org/resources/reading/documents/
TransitionGuide.pdf.

Horner, R. H., Carr, E. G., Strain, P. S., Todd, A. W., & Reed, H. K. (2002). Problem behavior interventions for young children with autism: A research synthesis. *Journal of Autism and Developmental Disorders, 32,* 423–446.

Howlin, P. (1998). Practitioner review: Psychological and educational treatments for autism. *Journal of Child Psychology and Psychiatry & Allied Disciplines, 39,* 307–322.

Individuals with Disabilities Education Improvement Act: Rules and Regulations, 71 Fed. Reg. 46540–46841 (August 16, 2006).

Iovannone, R., Dunlap, G., Huber, H., & Kincaid, D. (2003). Effective educational practices for students with autism spectrum disorders. *Focus on Autism and Other Developmental Disabilities, 18,* 150–165.

Jabarin, Z., Crocombe, J., Gralton, E., & Carter, S. (2001). Service innovations: Maple House—an autistic friendly NHS facility. *Psychiatric Bulletin, 25,* 109–111.

Jacobson, J. W., Mulick, J. A., & Green, G. (1998). Cost-benefit estimates for early intensive behavioral intervention for young children with autism: General model and single state case. *Behavioral Interventions, 13,* 201–226.

Johnson, C. P., Myers, S. M., & the Council on Children With Disabilities. (2007). Identification and evaluation of children with autism spectrum disorders. *Pediatrics, 120,* 1183–1215.

Jones, G. (2006). Department for Education and Skills/Department of Health good practice guidance on the education of children with autistic spectrum disorder. *Child: Care, Health, and Development, 32,* 543–552.

Kasari, C. (2002). Assessing change in early intervention programs for children with autism. *Journal of Autism and Developmental Disorders, 32,* 447–461.

Kleinman, J. M., Robins, D. L., Ventola, P. E., Pandey, J., Boorstein, H. C., Esser, E. L., et al. (2008). The Modified Checklist for Autism in Toddlers: A follow-up study investigating the early detection of autism spectrum disorders. *Journal of Autism and Developmental Disorders, 38,* 827–839.

Klin, A., Saulnier, C., Tsatsanis, K., & Volkmar, F. R. (2005). Clinical evaluation in autism spectrum disorders: Psychological assessment within a transdisciplinary framework. In F. R. Volkmar, R. Paul, A. Klin, & D. J. Cohen (Eds.), *Handbook of autism and pervasive developmental disorders, Volume 2: Assessment, interventions, and policy* (3rd ed., pp. 772–798). Hoboken, NJ: John Wiley & Sons.

Klinger, L. G., O'Kelley, S. E., & Mussey, J. L. (2009). Assessment of intellectual functioning in autism spectrum disorders. In S. Goldstein, J. A. Naglieri, & S. Ozonoff (Eds.), *Assessment of autism spectrum disorders* (pp. 209–252). New York: Guilford Press.

Klinger, L. G., & Williams, A. (2009). Cognitive-behavioral interventions for students with autism spectrum disorders. In M. J. Mayer, R. Van Acker, J. E. Lochman, & F. M. Gresham (Eds.), *Cognitive-behavioral interventions for emotional and behavioral disorders: School-based practice* (pp. 328–362). New York: Guilford Press.

Koegel, R. L., & Koegel, L. K. (2006). *Pivotal response treatments for autism: Communication, social, & academic development.* Baltimore: Brookes.

Koegel, R. L., Koegel, L. K., & McNerney, E. K. (2001). Pivotal areas in intervention for autism. *Journal of Clinical Child Psychology: Special Issue, 30,* 19–32.

Lavin, J. L. (2001). *Special kids need special parents: A resource for parents of children with special needs.* New York: Berkley.

Le Couteur, A., Lord, C., & Rutter, M. (2003). *Autism Diagnostic Interview-Revised.* Los Angeles: Western Psychological Services.

Lord, C., Risi, S., DiLavore, P. S., Shulman, C., Thurm, A., & Pickles, A. (2006). Autism from 2 to 9 years of age. *Archives of General Psychiatry, 63,* 694–701.

Lord, C., Risi, S., Lambrecht, L., Cook, E. H., Leventhal, B. L., DiLavore, P. C., et al. (2000). The Autism Diagnostic

Observation Schedule-Generic: A standard measure of social and communication deficits associated with the spectrum of autism. *Journal of Autism and Developmental Disorders, 30,* 205–223.

Lord, C., Risi, S., & Pickles, A. (2004). Trajectory of language development in autism spectrum disorders. In M. Rice & S. Warren (Eds.), *Developmental language disorders: From phenotypes to etiologies* (pp. 7–29). Mahwah, NJ: Erlbaum.

Lord, C., Rutter, M., DiLavore, P. C., & Risi, S. (1999). *Autism Diagnostic Observation Schedule.* Los Angeles: Western Psychological Services.

Lord, C., Rutter, M., & Le Couteur, A. (1994). Autism Diagnostic Interview-Revised: A revised version of a diagnostic interview for caregivers of individuals with possible pervasive developmental disorders. *Journal of Autism and Developmental Disorders, 24,* 659–685.

Lord, C., Wagner, A., Rogers, S., Szatmari, P., Aman, M., Charman, T., et al. (2005). Challenges in evaluating psycho-social interventions for autistic spectrum disorders. *Journal of Autism and Developmental Disorders, 35,* 695–708.

Losh, M., & Piven, J. (2007). Social-cognition and the broad autism phenotype: Identifying genetically meaningful phenotypes. *Journal of Child Psychology and Psychiatry, 48,* 105–112.

Lovaas, O. I. (1987). Behavioral treatment and normal educational and intellectual functioning in young autistic children. *Journal of Consulting and Clinical Psychology, 55,* 3–9.

Mandell, D. S., Ittenback, R. F., Levy, S. E., & Pinto-Martin, J. A. (2007). Disparities in diagnoses received prior to a diagnosis of autism spectrum disorder. *Journal of Autism and Developmental Disorders, 37,* 1795–1802.

Mandell, D. S., Novak, M. M., & Zubritsky, C. D. (2005). Factors associated with age of diagnosis among children with autism spectrum disorders. *Pediatrics, 116,* 1480–1486.

Mandlawitz, M. R. (2002). The impact of the legal system on educational programming for young children with autism spectrum disorder. *Journal of Autism and Developmental Disorders, 32,* 495–508.

Marcus, L., Kunce, L., & Schopler, E. (2005). Working with families. In F. Volkmar, R. Paul, A. Klin, & D. Cohen (Eds.), *Handbook of autism and pervasive developmental disorders, Volume 2: Assessment, interventions, and policy* (3rd ed., pp. 1055–1086). Hoboken, NJ: John Wiley & Sons.

Matson, J. L. (2007). Determining treatment outcome in early intervention programs for autism spectrum disorders: A critical analysis of measurement issues in learning based interventions. *Research in Developmental Disabilities, 28,* 207–218.

Matson, J. L., Matson, M. L., & Rivet, T. T. (2007). Social-skills treatments for children with autism spectrum disorders: An overview. *Behavior Modification, 31,* 682–707.

McConachie, H., & Diggle, T. (2007). Parent implemented early intervention for young children with autism spectrum disorder: A systematic review. *Journal of Evaluation in Clinical Practice, 13,* 120–129.

McConnell, S. R. (2002). Interventions to facilitate social interaction for young children with autism: Review of available research and recommendations for educational intervention and future research. *Journal of Autism and Developmental Disorders, 32,* 351–372.

McEachin, J. J., Smith, T., & Lovaas, O. I. (1993). Long-term outcome for children with autism who received early intensive behavioral treatment. *American Journal on Mental Retardation, 97,* 359–372.

Mundy, P., Delgado, C., Block, J., Venezia, M., Hogan, A., & Seibert, J. (2003). *A manual for the Abridged Early Social Communication Scales (ESCS).* Available through the University of Miami Psychology Department, Coral Gables, FL (pmundy@miami.edu).

Myers, S. M., Johnson, C. P., & the Council on Children With Disabilities. (2007). Management of children with autism spectrum disorders. *Pediatrics, 120,* 1162–1182.

Myles, B. S., Simpson, R. L., Ormsbee, C. K., & Erickson, C. (1993). Integrating preschool children with autism with their normally developing peers: Research findings and best practices recommendations. *Focus on Autistic Behavior, 8,* 1–18.

Naglieri, J. A., & Chambers, K. M. (2009). Psychometric issues and current scales for assessing autism spectrum disorders. In S. Goldstein, J. A. Naglieri, & S. Ozonoff (Eds.), *Assessment of autism spectrum disorders* (pp. 209–252). New York: Guilford Press.

National Research Council, Committee on Educational Interventions for Children With Autism (2001). *Educating children with autism.* Washington DC: National Academies Press.

New York State Department of Health, Division of Family Health Bureau of Early Intervention. (1999). *Clinical practice guideline: Quick reference guide for parents and professionals on autism/pervasive developmental disorders.* New York: Author.

No Child Left Behind Act of 2001, 20 U.S.C. § 6301 *et seq.* (2001).

O'Roak, B. J., & State, M. W. (2008). Autism genetics: Strategies, challenges, and opportunities. *Autism Research, 1,* 4–17.

Osterling, J., Dawson, G., & Munson, J. A. (2002). Early recognition of 1-year-old infants with autism spectrum disorder versus mental retardation. *Developmental Psychopathology, 14,* 239–251.

Ozonoff, S., Goodlin-Jones, B. L., & Solomon, M. (2007). Assessment of autism spectrum disorders. In E. J. Mash & R. A. Barkley (Eds.), *Assessment of childhood disorders* (4th ed.). New York: Guilford Press.

Ozonoff, S., Macari, S., Young, G. S., Goldring, S., Thompson, M., & Rogers, S. J. (2008). Atypical object exploration at 12 months of age is associated with autism in a prospective sample. *Autism, 12,* 457–472.

Ozonoff, S., South, M., & Miller, J. (2000). DSM-IV defined Asperger syndrome: Cognitive, behavioral and early history differentiation from high functioning autism. *Autism, 4,* 29–46.

Paul, R., & Wilson, K. P. (2009). Assessing speech, language, and communication in autism spectrum disorders. In S. Goldstein, J. A. Naglieri, & S. Ozonoff (Eds.), *Assessment of autism spectrum disorders* (pp. 209–252). New York: Guilford Press.

Robins, D., Fein, D., Barton, M., & Green, J. A. (2001). The Modified-Checklist for Autism in Toddlers (M-CHAT): An initial investigation in the early detection of autism and pervasive developmental disorders. *Journal of Autism and Developmental Disorders, 31,* 131–144.

Rodrigue, J. R., Geffken, G. R., & Morgan, S. B. (1993). Perceived competence and behavioral adjustment of siblings of children with autism. *Journal of Autism and Developmental Disorders, 23,* 665–674.

Rogers, S. J. (1998). Empirically supported comprehensive treatments of young children with autism. *Journal of Clinical Child Psychology, 27,* 168–179.

Rogers, S. J. (1999). Intervention for young children with autism: From research to practice. *Infants and Young Children, 12,* 1–16.

Rogers, S. J. (2000). Interventions that facilitate socialization in children with autism. *Journal of Autism and Developmental Disorders, 30,* 399–409.

Rogers, S. J., & Vismara, L. A. (2008). Evidence-based comprehensive treatments for early autism. *Journal of Clinical Child and Adolescent Psychology, 37,* 8–38.

Rogers, S. J., & Williams, J. H. G. (2006). *Imitation and the social mind: Autism and typical development.* New York: Guilford Press.

Rutter, M., Bailey, A., & Lord, C. (2003). *Social Communication Questionnaire.* Los Angeles: Western Psychological Services.

Schopler, E. (2001). Treatment for autism: From science to pseudo-science or anti-science. In E. Schopler, N. Yirmiya, C. Shulman, & L. Marcus (Eds.), *The research basis for autism intervention* (pp. 9–24). New York: Kluwer Academic/Plenum.

Schreibman, L. (2000). Intensive behavioral/psychoeducational treatments for autism: Research needs and future directions. *Journal of Autism and Developmental Disorders, 30,* 373–378.

Schreibman, L. (2005). *The science and fiction of autism.* Cambridge, MA: Harvard University Press.

Siegel, B. (2004). *The Pervasive Developmental Disorders Screening Test-II* (PDDST-II). San Antonio, TX: Harcourt Assessment.

Smith, T. (1996). Are other treatments effective? In C. Maurice, G. Green, & S. C. Luce (Eds.), *Behavioral intervention for young children with autism: A manual for parents and professionals* (pp. 45–59). Austin, TX: Pro-Ed.

Smith, T., & Perry, A. (2005). A sibling support group for brothers and sisters of children with autism. *Journal of Developmental Disabilities, 11,* 77–88.

Smith, T., Scahill, L., Dawson, G., Guthrie, D., Lord, C., Odom, S., et al. (2007). Designing research studies on psychosocial interventions in autism. *Journal of Autism and Developmental Disorders, 37,* 354–366.

Smith, S. W., Slattery, W. J., & Knopp, T. Y. (1993). Beyond the mandate: Developing individualized education programs that work for students with autism. *Focus on Autistic Behavior, 8,* 1–15.

Squires, J., Bricker, D., & Twombly, L. (2002). *The Ages and Stages Questionnaire: A parent completed child-monitoring system* (2nd ed.). Baltimore: Brookes.

Stone, W. L., Coonrod, E. E., & Ousley, O. Y. (2000). Brief report: Screening Tool for Autism in Two-Year-Olds (STAT): Development and preliminary data. *Journal of Autism and Developmental Disorders, 30,* 607–612.

Stone, W. L., Coonrod, E. E., Turner, L. M., & Pozdol, S. L. (2004). Psychometric properties of the STAT for early autism screening. *Journal of Autism and Developmental Disorders, 36,* 691–701.

Stone, W. L., McMahon, C. R., & Henderson, L. M. (2008). Use of the Screening Tool for Autism in Two-Year-Olds

(STAT) for children under 24 months: An exploratory study. *Autism, 12,* 557–573.

Tincani, M. (2007). Beyond consumer advocacy: Autism spectrum disorders, effective instruction, and public schools. *Intervention in School and Clinic, 43,* 47–51.

Tonge, B., Brereton, A., Kiomall, M., Mackinnon, A., King, N., & Rinehart, N. (2006). Effects on parental mental health of an education and skills training program for parents of young children with autism: A randomized controlled trial. *Journal of the American Academy of Child and Adolescent Psychiatry, 45,* 561–569.

Tuchman-Ginsburg, L., & Shaw, E. (2008, November). *National Professional Development Center on Autism Spectrum Disorders: Building our states' early identification and education systems.* Presentation at the meeting of the Network of Autism Training and Technical Assistance Programs (NATTAP), Columbus, OH.

Turner, L. M., Stone, W. L., Pozdol, S. L., & Coonrod, E. E. (2006). Follow up of children with autism spectrum disorders from age 2 to 9. *Autism, 10,* 257–269.

Van Bourgondien, M., Reichle, N., & Schopler, E. (2003). Effects of a model treatment approach on adults with autism. *Journal of Autism and Developmental Disorders, 33,* 133–140.

Verté, S., Roeyers, H., & Buysse, A. (2003). Behavioral problems, social competence, and self-concept in siblings of children with autism. *Child: Care, Health & Development, 29,* 193–205.

Volkmar, F., Cook, E. H., Pomeroy, J., Realmuto, G., & Tanguay, P. (1999). Practice parameters for the assessment and treatment of children, adolescents, and adults with autism and other pervasive developmental disorders. *Journal of the American Academy of Child and Adolescent Psychiatry, 38,* 32S–54S.

Wachtel, K., & Carter, A. S. (2008). Reaction to diagnosis and parenting styles among mothers of young children with ASDs. *Autism, 12,* 575–594.

Wetherby, A. M., Brosnan-Maddox, S., Peace, V., & Newton, L. (2008). Validation of the Infant-Toddler Checklist as a broadband screener for autism spectrum disorders from 9 to 24 months of age. *Autism, 12,* 487–511.

Wetherby, A. M., & Prizant, B. M. (2002). *Communication and Symbolic Behavior Scales Developmental Profile.* Baltimore: Brookes. Retrieved from http://firstwords.fsu.edu/pdf/checklist.pdf

Wetherby, A. M., & Woods, J. J. (2006). Early social interaction project for children with autism spectrum disorders beginning in the second year of life: A preliminary study. *Topics in Early Childhood Special Education, 26,* 67–82.

Wetherby, A. M., Woods, J., Allen, L., Cleary, J., Dickinson, H., & Lord, C. (2004). Early indicators of autism in the second year of life. *Journal of Autism and Developmental Disorders, 34,* 473–493.

White, S. W., Keonig, K., & Scahill, L. (2007). Social skills development in children with autism spectrum disorders: A review of the intervention research. *Journal of Autism and Developmental Disorders, 37,* 1858–1868.

Wilder, L. K., Dyches, T. T., Obiakor, F. E., & Algozzine, B. (2004). Multicultural perspectives on teaching students with autism. *Focus on Autism and Other Developmental Disabilities, 19,* 105–113.

Wolf, L., Fisman, S., Ellison, D., & Freeman, T. (1998). Effect of sibling perception of differential treatment in sibling dyads with one disabled child. *Journal of the American Academy of Child and Adolescent Psychiatry, 37,* 1317–1325.

World Health Organization. (1994). *International statistical classification of diseases and related health problems, 10th revision.* Geneva, Switzerland: Author.

Zwaigenbaum, L., Bryson, S., Lord, C., Rogers, S., Carter, A., Chawarska, K., et al. (2009). Clinical assessment and management of toddlers with suspected ASD: Insights from studies of high-risk infants. *Pediatrics, 123,* 1383–1391.

Sarah E. O'Kelley is a clinical psychology postdoctoral fellow at The University of Alabama at Birmingham Civitan-Sparks Clinics, where she is a member of the Autism Spectrum Disorders (ASD) training team. She also recently served as the program coordinator for The University of Alabama Autism Spectrum Disorders College Transition and Support program (UA-ACTS), a program she helped develop and implement. O'Kelley was a member of the Alabama Autism Collaborative Group and state-wide Needs Assessment team. She has been involved in research and treatment with individuals with ASD and their families for more than 10 years. She received her doctorate in clinical child psychology from The University of Alabama in 2006. O'Kelley's ASD research interests include cognitive and behavioral phenotypes of individuals with ASD, sibling and family functioning, group social skills interventions, and other issues across the lifespan. Her clinical interests include assessment and treatment with individuals with ASD, including cognitive and diagnostic assessment, individual and group therapy approaches, and school consultation.

Elizabeth McMahon Griffith has worked clinically and conducted research with individuals with autism spectrum disorders and their families for almost 20 years. She received her doctorate in clinical psychology from the University of Denver, where she specialized in neurodevelopmental disorders including autism through training at the University of Colorado Health Sciences Center. She currently is an assistant professor in the Department of Psychology at The University of Alabama at Birmingham and a psychologist at Civitan-Sparks Clinics. Griffith provides diagnostic and intervention services to children with ASD and their families. She runs an active research lab with ongoing projects in syndrome elaboration, the neurocognitive underpinnings of the symptoms of ASD, identification of the active ingredients in treatment, and the effective dissemination of a variety of evidence-based treatments. She has received research funding from both local and national sources, and frequently collaborates with researchers and providers in a variety of community based sites. She teaches at the graduate level and supervises trainees at all levels of experience both clinically and in research.

Laura Grofer Klinger is an associate professor in the Department of Psychology at The University of Alabama. She is the director of The University of Alabama Autism Spectrum Disorders Research Clinic and coordinator of the clinical child psychology graduate program. She is a clinical child psychologist whose research and clinical work focuses on autism spectrum disorders (ASD). Klinger received her Ph.D. in clinical psychology from the University of Washington and completed her clinical internship at the University of North Carolina. Klinger's research focuses on learning differences that underlie the social and language symptoms of ASD. She also conducts research examining the effectiveness of social skills interventions for individuals with ASD. She is a member of the editorial board for the *Journal of Abnormal Child Psychology* and has received grant funding through the National Institutes of Health. She teaches courses in lifespan development, psychological assessment, child psychotherapy, and autism spectrum disorders.

Sarah Ann McCurry is a fourth-year clinical psychology graduate student at The University of Alabama specializing in the diagnosis and treatment of autism spectrum disorders across the lifespan. Her research interests involve the development of early learning processes and implicit learning abilities in children with ASD. Clinically, her interests include the treatment of comorbid anxiety and high functioning autism. She also enjoys working with college students with Asperger's syndrome as a therapist-mentor for The University of Alabama Autism Spectrum Disorders College Transition and Support Program (UA-ACTS) and currently serves as graduate student coordinator for the program as well. McCurry served as a member of the Alabama Autism Collaborative Group and statewide Needs Assessment team.

Printed in the United States
by Baker & Taylor Publisher Services

Printed in the United States
by Baker & Taylor Publisher Services